HOW TO MAKE
SHAVING SOAP

CHARTING YOUR COURSE TO THE LAND OF LATHER

CARRIE SEIBERT

How to Make Shaving Soap: Charting Your Course to the Land of Lather
By Carrie Seibert

Editor: Anna J. Cooke
Managing Editor: Kayla Fioravanti
Cover Design: Jennifer Smith
Front Cover Photo: Jonathan Williquette
Back Cover Photo: Levi Seibert

ISBN-13: 978-0692795446 (Selah Press)
ISBN-10: 0692795448

Copyright © Carrie Seibert
Printed in the United States of America, Published by Selah Press, LLC

TABLE OF CONTENTS

CHAPTER 1

WELCOME ABOARD:
Introduction

Welcome Aboard! I'm glad you've joined me on this adventure to the Land of Lather. Creating an artisan shaving soap is somewhat like sailing. You're likely to experience sunny skies and pleasant surprises, alongside unexpected obstacles and, sometimes, choppy waters. And if you're setting sail for a new destination (or making your first batch of shaving soap), collecting all the pertinent and necessary information to chart your course can be confusing and time-consuming. I've done some of the legwork for you, by consolidating research and sharing my experience with shaving soap here in these pages.

This is a journey you won't have to take alone. I'm going to walk you through the process of envisioning, planning, formulating, and creating a high quality shaving soap. Taking the analogy of a ship, consider our ultimate destination to be the Land of Lather (located in the World of Wet Shaving) and the way to get there as being via shaving soap. As the commander of this ship, you get to call the shots and choose the course. Ready to cruise to a creamy lather? Read on!

CHAPTER 2

Buoys:
Cautions

Safety is paramount when making any type of soap. Having—and using—the appropriate protective gear (such as goggles, gloves, long sleeves, and closed-toe shoes) should be a non-negotiable. You will need to work in a safe, clean space that is free from distractions. Additionally, as with making any type of soap, be sure to use the appropriate tools and equipment. Chapter 5 *Grab Your Gear: Tools & Equipment* explores the specifics of this topic.

I highly recommend that you do not attempt making shaving soap until you are comfortable and competent at making bath soap via the cold process or hot process method. Experience and understanding the process will help you safely manage the temperatures and techniques required to make shaving soap.

CAUTION: If you have never made cold or hot process bath soap before (or are new at doing so), please see the RESOURCES section at the end of this book for suggested instructional material. Proper lye handing techniques are vital.

Handling Lye

Lye is a hazardous substance and should be treated carefully. It is safe for use in home soapmaking but some precautions must be taken. *The Soap Queen* Anne-Marie Faiola has given us permission to reprint her safe lye handling instructions.

Always wear protective goggles! Getting lye mixed with water or fresh soap in your eyes is an emergency. The best way to handle a lye emergency is to prevent it. If an accident does occur, immediately run your eye under cold water and seek medical help.

Always wear protective clothing. Once you mix your lye with water, it will heat up quickly due to a chemical reaction. If you splash or spill lye on your skin, you will get a chemical burn. Protect your hands with gloves, and wear long sleeved clothing.

Mix lye in a large heat-safe container, preferably inside a sink. If you prefer, you can mix your lye outdoors.

Always ADD LYE TO WATER. Sprinkle the lye on top of the water for best results, and stir with a stainless steel spoon or heat-resistant plastic utensil. Never pour water onto a pile of dry lye, as a severe, volcanic reaction can occur.

Work in a well-ventilated area and avoid breathing in lye fumes (these are strongest when you first add the lye to the water).

Do not allow children or pets into your soaping space while you are working.

Use dedicated soapmaking utensils and tools. Don't use your soap tools to make food.

In Case of a Lye Emergency

The following information is taken from the MSDS sheet for lye:

If swallowed:

Rinse mouth with water and drink one or two glasses of water. Do not induce vomiting! Immediately get medical attention or call your poison control center at 1-800-222-1222.

If in eyes:

Immediately flush eyes with water. Remove any contact lenses and continue to flush eyes with water for at least 20 minutes. Immediately get medical attention or call your poison control center at 1-800-222-1222.

If on skin:

Gently wipe product from skin and remove any contaminated clothing. Flush skin with plenty of water for at least 15 minutes and then wash thoroughly with soap and water. Contact a physician or call your poison control center at 1-800-222-1222.

CHAPTER 3
NEW TERRITORY:
The Land of Lather

Artisan shaving soaps are native to the Land of Lather—a strange province of Wet Shaving World, which consists mainly of men who are obsessed with reducing or removing facial hair in a traditional, old-school manner. Every day, citizens of Lather Land spend time fixated on which products to use, how voluminous a lather they can create, and whether their brothers in the wet shaving community have achieved the holy grail of shaving: BBS (baby butt smooth) without irritation.

As a shaving soap maker, your main objective is most likely to be a part of the Wet Shaving World and the first port of call is none other than the Land of Lather. Before trying to stake a claim in this new land, you'll want to invest the time and effort to learn the language and the customs of the natives. As this guide is focusing mainly on the shaving soap creation process, there isn't enough room to give a thorough overview of wet shaving as a whole. However, a few necessities demand your attention before going on: knowing the gear used for wet shaving and the different types of shaving soap. (For a quick intro into shave-speak, see the "Acronyms" section in the Appendix.)

The "gear" used for wet shaving typically falls into one of two categories: software and hardware. Razors (double-edged, single-edged, straight, shavette) and brushes (boar, badger, horse, synthetic) comprise the hardware side of things. Software covers products such as preshaves, aftershaves, balms, splashes, creams, and, of course, soap.

It's important to point out here that there is soap and then there is shaving soap, and the true, to-the-core wet shaver will not accept the first as a substitute for the second. Altering the formulation for regular bath soap (adding clay, increasing castor oil, decreasing olive oil, etc.) and trying to pass it off as shaving soap will invalidate your entry into the Land of Lather. True shaving soap necessitates a different approach and a fundamentally different form than that of a typical bar soap. What specific characteristics are needed? I'm glad you asked. Read on...

CHAPTER 4

MAP IT OUT:
Start With the End in Mind

If you're an experienced wet shaver, you'll probably want to skip ahead to the next section. However, if you're not a regular user of shaving soap, take some time to acquaint yourself with its desirable characteristics. After all, you want to make sure you chart a course that gets you to the right destination.

In the Land of Lather, Lather is King

A good artisan shaving soap will provide the following:

- Latherability—ability to create a voluminous lather by swirling a shaving brush over the surface of the soap (note: too many bubbles are bad!)

- Lather Stability—length of time that the lather will retain its form/shape before breaking down.

- Cushion/Protection—a moisturizing, comfortable layer of protection between the skin and the blade.

- Slip/Glide—ease with which the blade moves across the surface of the skin.

- Good Post Shave Feel—moisturized, nourished condition of the skin.

- Desirable Fragrance Level—robust and pleasing scent that is not too overpowering and remains within IFRA guidelines.

Creating (or building) a lather in the traditional manner of wet shaving can be a daunting and frustrating task. It's a tremendous help to watch someone lather soap, either in person or via video. If you don't live with a wet shaver or have any willing demonstrators close by, refer to the Appendix for a step-by-step tutorial on how to build a shave-ready lather. Alternatively, you can google "how to lather" or a close variation thereof and you'll have plenty of on-demand instructors.

CHAPTER 5
GRAB YOUR GEAR:
Tools & Equipment

Since you've already made handcrafted CP/HP bath soap (or you wouldn't be reading this far, right?), you most likely have all the necessary tools and equipment for creating shaving soap. Lye-safe containers, stainless steel or sturdy plastic buckets, non-wooden spoons, stick blenders, accurate scales…these are the basics. An infrared thermometer is very useful, especially since shaving soap utilizes high levels of stearic, which necessitates higher-than-average soaping temps.

In addition, you will need a heat source with which to melt your oils and keep them at a warm temperature. Depending on your method, this might be a crock-pot, hot plate, or induction cooktop. Most shaving soap is made via a traditional hot process method, but a modified cold process approach works also. (Both methods will be explained in Chapter 7 *Set Sail: A Basic Shaving Soap Recipe.*

One important factor to keep in mind is that the melting point of stearic acid is 157 degrees Fahrenheit, so if stearic is one of your ingredients you'll need to keep the temperature of your oils/butters mixture high enough for it to remain fully melted.

CAUTION: AGAIN If you are not familiar with the fundamentals of CP/HP soapmaking, please learn those before experimenting with shaving soap.

Before going on, I want to share two inexpensive tools that I find to be very helpful in shaving soap production. First are plastic (or stainless steel) canning funnels. These have a wide "mouth" and allow shaving soap containers to be filled more efficiently and effectively, making it a less messy affair. The second type of tools is a nylon pan scraper. Shaving soap residue can get firm quickly and pose a challenge to cleaning up. Handheld scrapers make the job much easier and do not damage your mixing vessels or working surface.

Containers & Molds

Shaving soap can be molded into a variety of containers. Many artisans prefer to pour/scoop the soap directly into the final tubs/jars. (Here's where the canning funnel comes in handy.) Others prefer to utilize individual cavity molds, while another option is a cylindrical or tube mold. If you opt to put the soap directly into its final container, make sure that the jar or tub is made out of a material that is safe for the mixture. (Aluminum tins are not a good choice as they will be exposed to a great deal of water, making even the coated ones prone to rust.)

If you will be offering your shaving soap in individual puck form, take into consideration the size of the container that the puck will be placed into. This will help determine the diameter of the cylindrical mold (or individual round cavity mold) you'll want to use.

CHAPTER 6

LEARN THE ROPES:
Building Blocks of a Quality Shaving Soap

Formulating a decent shaving soap is not difficult, but formulating an outstanding one requires more than just lucky guesses. As with any type of handcrafted soap, each ingredient will contribute to the overall characteristic and "persona" of the final product.

Shaving soap is no different. Choosing the right ingredients to meet your shaving soap goals is a piece of cake if you know the qualities you're aiming for and if you're familiar with what each ingredient brings to the table.

Of course it goes without saying that you don't have to know all the ins and outs of fatty acid profiles and lye ratios in order to actually make a shaving soap. You can choose to follow a pre-made, basic recipe and get good results. It's like getting in your car, driving straight to your destination, and not looking out the side windows. Most people would find that boring, but effective. If that's your desire, don your soapmaking gear and flip over to the next chapter.

However, I hope you'll choose to slow down and learn the ropes, as we explore the characteristics and profiles of various shaving soap ingredients. It won't take long, and your soap will be the better for it.

A Note about Lye and Shaving Soap

A hallmark of shaving soap, and one of the main factors, which distinguishes a true shaving soap from traditional bath soap, is the presence of potassium hydroxide (KOH). Potassium hydroxide delivers a softer consistency in shaving soap and often makes it easier to lather than a pure NaOH soap (depending on the ingredients used). For these reasons, some shaving soaps will employ KOH as the sole lye in their formulation. Most typically, though, a combination of both KOH and NaOH are used, as they work synergistically to achieve optimal texture, consistency, and latherability.

It is best to choose your ingredients first and then experiment with the proportions of the dual lyes. A standard starting point is to use 60% KOH and 40% NaOH, though you may find that a different ratio is more advantageous for your formulation. Chapter 8 *Adjust the Sails: Variations on the Basic Recipe* contains more detail regarding how to calculate dual lye amounts, so be sure to read and understand that section before attempting to formulate your own recipe or alter an existing one.

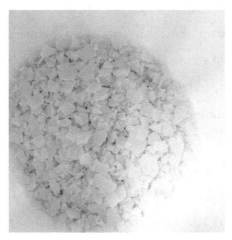

General Properties of a Shaving Soap Recipe

As with all soap, there are exceptions to the "rules," and some soaps don't look promising on paper but perform in a way that far exceeds expectations. I like to use the calculator at SoapCalc.net to create recipes and numerically evaluate the characteristics of the soap. Generally speaking, a good shaving soap recipe will have a LOW cleansing number, but a HIGH creamy factor. Additionally, when examining the fatty acid profile, you'll want to aim for a HIGH stearic/palmitic count (combined score of 50+ is best).

Fatty Acid	Contribution to Shaving Soap
Stearic	Dense, thick, creamy, stable lather
Palmitic	Stable, creamy lather
Lauric/Myristic	Fluffy lather (volume); cleansing
Oleic/Linoleic/Linolenic	Conditioning (lather killer)
Ricinoleic	Moisturizing, fluffy/stable lather (too much can weigh down the lather)

While most any oil/butter can be used in shaving soap, there are a select group of fats that are most commonly chosen:

Ingredient	Effect in Shaving Soap
Stearic Acid	Dense, creamy, stable lather
Coconut Oil	A small amount helps with working the lather, but too much is drying and overly cleansing
Glycerin	Lubricant, humectant, slickness, moisturizing
Mango/Kokum/Shea/ Cocoa Butter	Contributes good stearic amounts; creaminess
Palm Oil	Stable, creamy lather
Tallow/Lard	Contains palmitic and stearic acids, but also a decent amount of oleic. Thus, it gives conditioning and moisturization, but too much may challenge the lather.
Castor Oil	Conditioning; creamy/stable lather

For specific information about the fatty acid profiles of each ingredient, consult a reputable chart such as the ones referenced in the RESOURCES section at the end of this book.

CHAPTER 7

SET SAIL:
A Basic Shaving Soap Recipe

And finally...preparations are complete and you're ready to set sail. Time to make some shaving soap!

Some of you have jumped directly to this chapter, skipping pretty much everything prior to this point. (Yep, I might have done the same thing.) If this applies to you, I encourage you to go ahead and make the recipe here and then flip back to the beginning of this book and actually read it. If you know all the information already, great! You've had a quick refresher course. On the other hand, there are likely to be some valuable nuggets in the previous chapters that might help you understand the soapmaking process more thoroughly or better equip you as you formulate your own recipe.

Before we get to the nitty-gritty of the recipe, you'll need to choose which method you want to use: Traditional Hot Process or Modified Cold Process. Always prepare your soaping area and gather all necessary equipment, tools, containers, and ingredients. Read through the entire recipe and instructions prior to starting the soapmaking process.

32 ounce Sample Recipe			
Oils/Fat	**%**	**Ounces**	**Grams**
Stearic acid	60%	19.2	544
Coconut oil	20%	6.4	181
Shea butter	15%	4.8	136
Castor oil	5%	1.6	45
Lyes			
Potassium hydroxide (KOH)	60%	4.15	118
Sodium hydroxide (NaOH)	40%	1.75	50
Other			
Distilled water		12.15	344
Glycerin (optional)		3.2	90
Fragrance (optional)		1-1.4	28-30

CAUTION: Before beginning, be sure to choose a crockpot or container for mixing that is large enough to accommodate a rising amount of soap. When the lye water hits the oils there is the chance for a small volcano. You'll want a vessel with plenty of room for it to expand and be stirred down.

HOT PROCESS METHOD

1. Suit up! When making soap, always wear goggles, gloves, closed-toe shoes, and long sleeves.

2. Melt oils/fats in a crock-pot. Bring temperature to between 160 and 170 degrees Fahrenheit.

3. Measure the correct amounts of lye and water into appropriate containers. Carefully add the lye to the water, stirring gently and thoroughly. Stir until solution is clear.

4. Carefully pour lye water into warmed oils.

5. Blend with stick blender until combined. Your mixture may be thick (similar to mashed potatoes) almost instantly.

6. Keep crock-pot on low, with top cover on, to prevent evaporation.

7. Let the soap rest for 15-20 minutes, then stir mixture together by hand.

8. Repeat Step 7 two or three times, keeping an eye on the mixture so that it does not overheat and grow out of the crock-pot (temps should not reach higher than 200 degrees Fahrenheit).

9. Once the soap is finished cooking (usually around 1 hour), stir in fragrance, glycerin, and/or other additives. Be careful not to stir too quickly or vigorously, as the glycerin may cause the batter to slosh or slide around inside the crock pot.

10. Scoop soap into containers or mold. If placing soap into containers/tubs, allow the soap to cool completely before covering. Placing lids on the containers too early may create excessive moisture or high temperatures.

MODIFIED COLD PROCESS METHOD

1. Suit up! When making soap, always wear goggles, gloves, closed-toe shoes, and long sleeves.

2. Measure the correct amount of all oils and fats. Combine the oils/fats and carefully warm to between 160 and 170 degrees Fahrenheit.

3. If using glycerin and fragrance or essential oil, measure these now and set them aside for Step 7.

4. Measure the correct amounts of lye(s) and water into appropriate containers. Carefully add the lye to the water, stirring gently and thoroughly until solution is clear.

5. When lye water is between 150 and 180 degrees Fahrenheit, slowly pour lye water into oils/butters.

6. Use a stick blender to mix until the lye water and the oils are completely combined. Your mixture may be thick (similar to mashed potatoes) almost instantly, or it may take up to a minute for the mixture to pull together and become homogeneous.

7. Stir in glycerin and fragrance (if using). Continue stirring by hand until these additives are well-incorporated and the mixture does not separate. Be careful not to stir too quickly or vigorously, as the glycerin may cause the batter to slosh or slide around in the container initially.

8. Stir by hand until soap becomes thinner and smoother, typically between 2-10 minutes. You do not need to stir continuously, as it is fine to allow the soap to rest for a few minutes as long as you keep an eye on it to observe any changes. (Temperature, fragrance, and essential oil can each have varying effects on the consistency of the soap at this stage.) If your soap does not become thinned-out and shiny during this time, but remains cohesive and not separated, proceed with the next step.

9. Depending on the thickness of your mixture, either pour or scoop the soap into a mold or heat-safe containers. Be sure to verify that the temperature tolerances of the containers or mold are appropriate for high-heat mixtures. (Containers labeled PP are one safe option.) Gently tap containers on a firm surface to help reduce air pockets.

10. If pouring into individual containers/tubs, allow the soap to cool completely before covering. Placing lids on the containers too early may create excessive moisture or high temperatures.

Choosing between the CP and HP methods of making shaving soap is merely a matter of familiarity and preference. If you typically make bath soap via the Cold Process method, then try out the CP approach to making shaving soap first. Vice versa for those of you who are more comfortable with Hot Process. Either way, it's a good idea to begin with the method you're most familiar with and then challenge yourself to create shaving soap by an alternative approach. I've made the recipes in this book via both methods and have found no difference in the end result, regardless of the method used.

CHAPTER 8

ADJUST THE SAILS:
Variations on the Basic Recipe

Now that you've successfully made a real shaving soap, it's time to explore a bit. Refer back to Chapter 6 *Learn the Ropes: Building Blocks of a Quality Shaving Soap* as a reminder of the characteristics and contributions of various ingredients and fatty acids. Additionally, before altering any soap recipe, be sure to familiarize yourself with a dependable lye calculator, such as SoapCalc. (See RESOURCES at the end of this book for additional lye calculator suggestions.)

REMINDER: When you alter any ingredient in a recipe, you must run the data through a lye calculator to attain the correct (and safe) amount of lye for your recipe. Do not assume that a similar oil/butter will require the same amount of lye for saponification.

General Guidelines:

- A good place to begin experimenting with dual lyes is 60% KOH, 40% NaOH.

- Start with a superfat of 5% and adjust to find a good level for your recipe.

- Do not try to discount your water; use the full water amount. This is traditionally designated as a lye concentration of 26% - 30%. (On SoapCalc, the value for "Water as % of Oils" should be preset at 38 for full water.) Another easy way to estimate the amount of water to use is to add up the total amount of lye and multiply by 2 or 2.2. This will give you a reasonable amount of water to work with.

 **NOTE:** Most commercially available Potassium Hydroxide is 90% pure. SoapCalc is one lye calculator that allows you to make that designation in your recipe characteristics and calculates accordingly. The Bramble Berry lye calculator assumes 90% purity for the KOH.

STEPS TO CREATING A DUAL LYE SHAVING SOAP RECIPE (WITH A STANDARD LYE CALCULATOR):

1. Choose the oils/fats for your recipe and determine the percentages of each. (The total percentages of the oils/fats need to add up to 100.)

2. Decide on the size of your batch.

3. Decide the percentages for KOH and NaOH that you want to use. (The total percentages of your lyes need to add up to 100. A typical place to begin experimenting is 60% KOH and 40% NaOH.)

4. Using a lye calculator, determine the amount of KOH required for the recipe. (This is **NOT** the amount of KOH you will use for your final recipe.)

5. Run the exact same recipe through the lye calculator, choosing NaOH as the lye this time. (This is **NOT** the amount of NaOH you will use for your final recipe.)

6. To determine the KOH needed for the final recipe: Take the amount you got in Step 4 and multiply it by the decimal equivalent of the percent of KOH you want in your shaving soap. (Remember that the decimal equivalent of a percent will be the percentage with the decimal place moved two spaces to the left. For example, 60% is represented as .60; likewise 40% is represented as .40) So if the lye calculator calls for 6.5 oz. of KOH and you want to have a recipe with 60% KOH, you need to multiply 6.5 x .6 for a total of 3.9 ounces.

7. To determine the NaOH needed for the final recipe, follow a process similar to Step 6: Take the NaOH amount from Step 5 and multiply it by the decimal equivalent of the percent of NaOH you want in your shaving soap. For example, if the lye calculator calls for 4.5 ounces of NaOH and you have a recipe with 40% NaOH, you will multiply 4.5 x .4 for a total of 1.8.

8. If using additives such as glycerin or sodium lactate, calculate the amounts needed as percentages of the total oil/fats weight.

Additional Ideas for Tweaking a Recipe:

- Replace the water with aloe vera juice, milk, or alcohol.

- Change the lye ratio or use potassium hydroxide only.

- Use lanolin as an ingredient. (Remember to adjust your % of oils/butters, as lanolin is considered saponifiable.)

CHAPTER 9

ALTERNATE ROUTES:
Additional Recipes

Need a good launch point? You've come to the right place. This chapter provides 10 additional recipes to get you headed in the right direction. After each recipe is a blank section to use as a record, or log, of your experience with that soap. Data such as temperature, behavior of the batter, fragrance used, timing, etc., as well as the performance of the final soap, should be notated.

The formulations in this chapter have some common characteristics:

- Calculations for a 2 pound (32 ounce) batch of soap.
- 90% purity is assumed for the Potassium Hydroxide calculations. When dual lyes are used, the standard 60/40 split is used for KOH/NaOH.
- Each recipe includes the option of glycerin (at 10% of the total oils/fats) as well as fragrance, with a suggested usage rate of 0.5 to 0.7 ounces per pound oil (PPO).
- Instructions are given for a modified cold process method.
- All recipes include a 5% superfat.

Before beginning, prepare your soaping area and gather all necessary equipment, tools, containers, and ingredients. Read through the entire recipe and instructions prior to starting the soapmaking process.

Recipe 1			
A simple combination of stearic acid and coconut oil.			
Oils/Fat	**%**	**Ounces**	**Grams**
Stearic acid	80%	25.6	725
Coconut oil	20%	6.4	181
Lyes			
Potassium hydroxide (KOH)	60%	4.25	120
Sodium hydroxide (NaOH)	40%	1.8	51
Other			
Distilled water		12.15	344
Glycerin (optional)		3.2	90
Fragrance (optional)		1-1.14	28-40

1. Suit up! When making soap, always wear goggles, gloves, closed-toe shoes, and long sleeves.

2. Measure the correct amount of stearic acid and coconut oil. Combine the stearic and coconut, and carefully warm to between 160 and 170 degrees Fahrenheit.

3. If using glycerin and fragrance or essential oil, measure these now and set them aside for Step 7.

4. Measure the correct amounts of both lyes and water into appropriate containers. Carefully add the lyes to the water, stirring gently and thoroughly. Stir until solution is clear.

5. When lye water is between 150 and 180 degrees Fahrenheit, slowly pour lye water into the warm stearic-coconut mixture.

6. Use a stick blender to mix until the lye water and the oils are completely combined and resemble mashed potatoes. Your mixture may be thick almost instantly, or it may take up to a minute for the mixture to pull together and become homogeneous.

7. Stir in glycerin and fragrance (if using). Continue stirring by hand until these additives are well-incorporated and the mixture does not separate. Be careful not to stir too quickly or vigorously, as the glycerin may cause the batter to slosh or slide around in the container initially.

8. Continue stirring until soap reaches a thinned-out, Vaseline-type stage. This is typically anywhere from 2-10 minutes. Temperature, fragrance, and essential oil can each have varying effects on the consistency of the soap at this stage. If your soap does not become thinned-out and shiny, allow it to rest for a few minutes and then stir again. If it stays thick, proceed with the next step.

9. Depending on the thickness of your mixture, either pour or scoop the soap into a mold or heat-safe containers. Be sure to verify that the temperature tolerances of the containers or mold are appropriate for

high-heat mixtures. (Containers labeled PP are one safe option.) Gently tap containers on a firm surface to help reduce air pockets.

10. If pouring into individual containers/tubs, allow the soap to cool completely before covering. Placing lids on the containers too early may create excessive moisture or high temperatures.

Recipe 1 LOG

Date:

Notes:

Recipe 2			
A butter-rich, single-lye vegan combination.			
Oils/Fat	**%**	**Ounces**	**Grams**
Stearic acid	38%	12.15	345
Shea Butter	14%	4.5	127
Kokum Butter	14%	4.5	127
Coconut Oil	10%	3.2	91
Castor Oil	10%	3.2	91
Avocado Oil	10%	3.2	91
Sunflower Oil	4%	1.3	36
Lyes			
Potassium hydroxide (KOH)	100%	6.65	188
Other			
Distilled water		12.15	344
Glycerin (optional)		3.2	90
Fragrance (optional)		1-1.4	28-40

1. Suit up! When making soap, always wear goggles, gloves, closed-toe shoes, and long sleeves.

2. Measure the correct amount of all oils and fats (stearic acid, shea butter, kokum butter, coconut oil, castor oil, avocado oil, and sunflower oil). Combine the oils/fats and carefully warm to between 160 and 170 degrees Fahrenheit.

3. If using glycerin and fragrance or essential oil, measure these now and set them aside for Step 7.

4. Measure the correct amount of potassium hydroxide (KOH) and water into appropriate containers. Carefully add the lye to the water, stirring gently and thoroughly. Stir until solution is clear.

5. When lye water is between 150 and 180 degrees Fahrenheit, slowly pour lye water into the warmed oil mixture.

6. Use a stick blender to mix until the lye water and the oils are completely combined. Your mixture may be thick almost instantly. Don't be concerned if it takes up to a minute or two for the mixture to pull together and become homogeneous.

7. Stir in glycerin and fragrance (if using). Continue stirring by hand until these additives are well-incorporated and the mixture does not separate. Be careful not to stir too quickly or vigorously, as the glycerin may cause the batter to slosh or slide around in the container initially.

8. This recipe typically requires some extra stirring. You do not need to stir continuously! Stir for a while and let the mixture sit for a few seconds or up to a minute before stirring again. Your goal is to reach a thinned-out, Vaseline-type stage. This is typically anywhere from 2-10 minutes, and can be effected by temperature, fragrance, or essential oil. However, if your soap stays thick even after 10 minutes of stirring and waiting, proceed with the next step.

9. Depending on the thickness of your mixture, either pour or scoop the soap into a mold or heat-safe containers. Be sure to verify that the temperature tolerances of the containers or mold are appropriate for high-heat mixtures. (Containers labeled PP are one safe option.) Gently tap containers on a firm surface to help reduce air pockets.

10. If pouring into individual containers/tubs, allow the soap to cool completely before covering. Placing lids on the containers too early may create excessive moisture or high temperatures.

Recipe 2 LOG

Date:

Notes:

Recipe 3			
Butter, butter, and more butter dominate this formulation.			
Oils/Fat	**%**	**Ounces**	**Grams**
Stearic acid	40%	12.8	363
Shea Butter	20%	6.4	181
Kokum Butter	20%	6.4	181
Cocoa Butter	15%	4.8	136
Castor Oil	5%	1.6	45
Lyes			
Potassium hydroxide (KOH)	60%	3.85	109
Sodium hydroxide (NaOH)	40%	1.65	47
Other			
Distilled water		12.15	344
Glycerin (optional)		3.2	90
Fragrance (optional)		1-1.4	28-40

Before beginning, read through the entire recipe and instructions. Prepare your soaping area and gather all necessary equipment, tools, containers, and ingredients prior to starting the soapmaking process.

1. Suit up! When making soap, always wear goggles, gloves, closed-toe shoes, and long sleeves.

2. Measure the correct amount of all oils and butters (stearic acid, shea butter, kokum butter, cocoa butter, and castor oil). Combine the

oils/butters and carefully warm the mixture to between 160 and 170 degrees Fahrenheit.

3. If using glycerin and fragrance or essential oil, measure these now and set them aside for Step 7.

4. Measure the correct amounts of potassium hydroxide (KOH), sodium hydroxide (NaOH), and water into separate containers. Carefully add the lyes to the water, stirring gently and thoroughly. Stir until solution is clear.

5. When lye water is between 150 and 180 degrees Fahrenheit, slowly pour lye water into oils/butters.

6. Mix with a stick blender until the lye water and the oils are completely combined. Your mixture may thicken quickly, or it may take up to a minute or more for the mixture to pull together and become homogeneous. If the mixture looks separated, continue to blend.

7. Stir in glycerin and fragrance (if using). Continue stirring by hand until these additives are well-incorporated and the mixture does not separate. (Be careful not to stir too quickly or vigorously, as the glycerin may cause the batter to slosh or slide around in the container initially.)

8. Stir the mixture by hand until soap becomes thinner and translucent. You do not need to stir continuously, as sometimes letting the soap sit

for a minute or two between stirring times encourages it to thin out and become more pourable. This part of the process typically takes anywhere from 2-10 minutes. (Temperature, fragrance, and essential oil can each have varying effects on the consistency of the soap at this stage.) If, after stirring and waiting, your soap stays thick, proceed with the next step.

9. Depending on the thickness of your mixture, either pour or scoop the soap into a mold or heat-safe containers. Be sure to verify that your containers or molds can tolerate the high-heat of the soap mixture. (Containers labeled PP are one safe option.) Gently tap containers on a firm surface to help reduce air pockets.

10. If pouring into individual containers/tubs, allow the soap to cool completely before covering. Placing lids on the containers too early may create excessive moisture or high temperatures.

Recipe 3 LOG
Date:

Notes:

Recipe 4			
A traditional vegan recipe, with babassu oil taking the place of coconut oil for a small amount of bubblage.			
Oils/Fat	**%**	**Ounces**	**Grams**
Stearic acid	50%	16	454
Shea Butter	15%	4.8	136
Cocoa Butter	15%	4.8	136
Babassu Oil	10%	3.2	91
Avocado Oil	5%	1.6	45
Castor Oil	5%	1.6	45
Lyes			
Potassium hydroxide (KOH)	60%	4	113
Sodium Hydroxide (NaOH)	40%	1.7	48
Other			
Distilled water		12.15	344
Glycerin (optional)		3.2	90
Fragrance (optional)		1-1.4	28-40

Prepare your soaping area and gather all necessary equipment, tools, containers, and ingredients before beginning. Read through the entire recipe and instructions prior to starting the soapmaking process.

1. Suit up! When soaping, always wear goggles, gloves, closed-toe shoes, and long sleeves.

2. Measure the correct amounts of stearic acid, shea butter, cocoa

butter, babassu oil, avocado oil, and castor oil. Combine the oils/fats and carefully warm to between 160 and 170 degrees Fahrenheit.

3. If using glycerin and fragrance or essential oil, measure these now and set them aside for Step 7.

4. Measure the correct amounts of the two lyes (KOH and NaOH) and water into appropriate containers. Carefully add the lyes to the water, stirring gently and thoroughly, until the solution is clear.

5. When lye water is between 150 and 180 degrees Fahrenheit, slowly pour lye water into oils/butters.

6. Using a stick blender, mix until the lye water and the oils are completely combined. Sometimes the mixture looks like mashed potatoes almost instantly, or it may take up to a minute for the mixture to pull together and become homogeneous.

7. Stir in glycerin and fragrance (if using). Continue stirring by hand until these additives are well-incorporated and the mixture does not separate. (The glycerin may cause the batter to slosh or slide around in the container initially so be careful not to stir too quickly or vigorously.)

8. Continue stirring until soap becomes thinner. Temperature, fragrance, and essential oil can each have varying effects on the consistency of the soap at this stage and the stirring process can take

anywhere from 2 to 10 minutes. If your soap does not become thinned-out and shiny, allow it to rest for a few minutes and then stir again. If it stays thick, proceed with the next step.

9. Pour (or scoop) the soap into a mold or heat-safe containers. Be sure to verify that the temperature tolerances of the containers or mold are appropriate for high-heat mixtures. (Containers labeled PP are one safe option.) Gently tap containers on a firm surface to help reduce air pockets.

10. If pouring into individual containers/tubs, allow the soap to cool completely before covering. Placing lids on the containers too early may create excessive moisture or high temperatures.

Recipe 4 LOG

Date:

Notes:

Recipe 5			
High stearic acid, supported by babassu and avocado oils.			
Oils/Fat	**%**	**Ounces**	**Grams**
Stearic acid	75%	24	680
Babassu Oil	15%	4.8	136
Avocado Oil	5%	1.6	45
Castor Oil	5%	1.6	45
Lyes			
Potassium hydroxide (KOH)	60%	4.1	117
Sodium Hydroxide (NaOH)	40%	1.75	50
Other			
Distilled water		12.15	344
Glycerin (optional)		3.2	90
Fragrance (optional)		1-1.4	28-40

Read through the entire recipe and instructions prior to starting the soapmaking process. Then prepare your work area and gather all necessary equipment, tools, containers, and ingredients.

1. Suit up! When making soap, always wear goggles, gloves, closed-toe shoes, and long sleeves.

2. Measure out the correct amounts of stearic acid, babassu oil, avocado oil, and castor oil. Combine the oils/fats and carefully warm the mixture to between 160 and 170 degrees Fahrenheit.

3. If using glycerin and fragrance or essential oil, measure these now and set them aside for Step 7.

4. Measure the correct amounts of both lyes into an appropriate container and measure the correct amount of water into a separate containers. Carefully add the lye to the water, stirring gently and thoroughly, until the solution is clear.

5. When lye water is between 150 and 180 degrees Fahrenheit, slowly pour lye water into oils/butters.

6. Use a stick blender to mix until the lye water and the oils resemble mashed potatoes. Your mixture may be thick almost instantly, or it may take up to a minute for the mixture to pull together and become homogeneous.

7. Stir in glycerin and fragrance (if using). Continue stirring by hand until these additives are well-incorporated and the mixture does not separate. (If you stir too vigorously the glycerin may cause the batter to slosh or slid around in the container, so be careful.)

8. Continue stirring the soap for 2-10 minutes. (You do not need to stir continuously during this part of the process. It is fine to let it rest for a minute or two in between stirring sessions.) Typically, the soap reaches a thinned-out, Vaseline-type stage, although temperature, fragrance, and essential oil can each have varying effects on the consistency of the soap at this stage. If your soap does not become thinned-out and shiny,

allow it to rest for a few more minutes and then stir again. If it stays thick like mashed potatoes, proceed with the next step.

9. Before filling your jars or molds, verify the heat-tolerance of the container. (Containers labeled PP are one safe option.) Depending on the thickness of your mixture, either pour or scoop the soap into the mold or jars and gently tap the container(s) on a firm surface to help reduce air pockets.

10. If pouring into individual containers/tubs, allow the soap to cool completely before covering. Placing lids on the containers too early may create excessive moisture or high temperatures.

Recipe 5 LOG

Date:

Notes:

Recipe 6			
A tallow-based soap, loaded with butters.			
Oils/Fat	**%**	**Ounces**	**Grams**
Beef Tallow	30%	9.6	272
Stearic Acid	30%	9.6	272
Shea Butter	15%	4.8	136
Kokum Butter	15%	4.8	136
Sunflower Oil	5%	1.6	45
Castor Oil	5%	1.6	45
Lyes			
Potassium hydroxide (KOH)	60%	3.9	111
Sodium Hydroxide (NaOH)	40%	1.65	47
Other			
Distilled water		12.15	344
Glycerin (optional)		3.2	90
Fragrance (optional)		1-1.4	28-40

Before beginning, prepare your soaping area and gather all necessary equipment, tools, containers, and ingredients. Read through the entire recipe and instructions prior to starting the soapmaking process.

1. Suit up! When making soap, always wear goggles, gloves, closed-toe shoes, and long sleeves.

2. Measure the correct amount of all oils and fats (beef tallow, stearic acid, shea butter, kokum butter, sunflower oil, and castor oil). Combine

the oils/fats and carefully warm the mixture to between 160 and 170 degrees Fahrenheit.

3. If using glycerin and fragrance or essential oil, measure these now and set them aside for Step 7.

4. Measure the correct amounts of potassium hydroxide and sodium hydroxide into an appropriate container, and measure the water into a separate container. Carefully add the lyes to the water, stirring gently and thoroughly. Stir until solution is clear.

5. When lye water is between 150 and 180 degrees Fahrenheit, slowly pour lye water into the warmed oils/fats.

6. Using a stick blender, mix until the lye water and the oils are completely combined. It may take a minute or more for the mixture to pull together and become homogeneous. Continue to use the stick blender until you feel confident that the mixture is not going to separate.

7. Stir in glycerin and fragrance (if using). Be careful not to stir too quickly or vigorously, as the addition of the glycerin may cause the batter to slosh or slide around in the container initially. Continue stirring by hand until these additives are well-incorporated and the mixture does not separate.

8. Continue stirring by hand, from 2-10 minutes, taking breaks as needed. Temperature, fragrance, and essential oil can each have varying effects on the consistency of the soap at this stage, but you are looking for the soap to become thinner. However, if your soap does not become thinned-out and shiny, allow it to rest for a few minutes and then stir again. If it stays thick, just proceed with the next step.

9. Depending on the thickness of your mixture, either pour or spoon the soap into a mold or heat-safe containers. Be sure to verify that the temperature tolerances of the containers or mold are appropriate for high-heat mixtures. (Containers labeled PP are one safe option.) Gently tap containers on a firm surface to help reduce air pockets.

10. If pouring into individual containers/tubs, allow the soap to cool completely before covering. Placing lids on the containers too early may create excessive moisture or high temperatures.

Recipe 6 LOG

Date:

Notes:

Recipe 7			
This tallow-based soap is free of stearic acid and coconut.			
Oils/Fat	**%**	**Ounces**	**Grams**
Beef Tallow	30%	9.6	272
Palm Oil	25%	8	227
Kokum Butter	25%	8	227
Shea Butter	20%	6.4	181
Lyes			
Potassium hydroxide (KOH)	60%	3.9	111
Sodium Hydroxide (NaOH)	40%	1.65	47
Other			
Distilled water		12.15	344
Glycerin (optional)		3.2	90
Fragrance (optional)		1-1.4	28-40

Before beginning, read through the entire recipe and instructions. Prepare your soaping area and gather all necessary equipment, tools, containers, and ingredients prior to starting the soapmaking process.

1. Suit up! When making soap, always wear goggles, gloves, closed-toe shoes, and long sleeves.

2. Measure out the correct amounts of beef tallow, palm oil, kokum butter, and shea butter. Combine these ingredients and carefully warm to between 160 and 170 degrees Fahrenheit.

3. If using glycerin and fragrance or essential oil, measure these now and set them aside for Step 7.

4. Weigh out the correct amounts of both lyes into an appropriate container. Weigh out the correct amount of water into a separate container. Carefully add the lye to the water, stirring gently and thoroughly, until solution is clear.

5. When lye water is between 150 and 180 degrees Fahrenheit, slowly pour lye water into oils/butters.

6. Use a stick blender to mix until the lye water and the oils are completely combined. Due to the absence of stearic acid as an ingredient in this recipe, this step in the process may take longer than usual. Continue to stick blend (taking short breaks as needed so as not to overheat the blender) until the mixture pulls together and becomes homogeneous.

7. Stir in glycerin and fragrance (if using). Continue stirring by hand until these additives are well-incorporated and the mixture does not separate. Be careful not to stir too quickly or vigorously, as the glycerin may cause the batter to slosh or slide around in the container initially.

8. Stir soap by hand for an additional 2-10 minutes, letting the soap rest occasionally. During this time your soap may thicken like mashed potatoes and then thin out to a Vaseline-type consistency. (Temperature, fragrance, and essential oil can all effect the reaction of

the soap during this stage.) If your soap stays thin, make sure you continue to work with it until you are certain you have reached trace. Contrarily, if your soap is very thick, allow it to rest for a few minutes and then stir again. Many times this will encourage the soap to become more thinned-out and shiny. However, if it stays thick, simply proceed with the next step.

9. Prior to filling a mold or containers with hot soap, be sure to verify that the temperature tolerances of the containers or mold are appropriate for high-heat mixtures. (Containers labeled PP are one safe option.) Depending on the thickness of your mixture, either pour or spoon the soap into the mold/containers. Gently tap containers on a firm surface to help reduce air pockets.

10. If pouring into individual containers/tubs, allow the soap to cool completely before covering. Placing lids on the containers too early may create excessive moisture or high temperatures.

Recipe 7 LOG

Date:

Notes:

Recipe 8

A typical stearic acid based soap, supported by skin loving tallow and butters.

Oils/Fat	%	Ounces	Grams
Stearic acid	50%	16	454
Beef Tallow	20%	6.4	181
Kokum Butter	10%	3.2	91
Shea Butter	10%	3.2	91
Coconut Oil	5%	1.6	45
Castor Oil	5%	1.6	45
Lyes			
Potassium hydroxide (KOH)	60%	4	113
Sodium Hydroxide (NaOH)	40%	1.7	48
Other			
Distilled water		12.15	344
Glycerin (optional)		3.2	90
Fragrance (optional)		1-1.4	28-40

Before beginning, prepare your soaping area and gather all necessary equipment, tools, containers, and ingredients. Read through the entire recipe and instructions prior to starting the soapmaking process.

1. Suit up! When making soap, always wear goggles, gloves, closed-toe shoes, and long sleeves.

2. Weigh out the correct amount of all oils and fats, including stearic

acid, beef tallow, kokum butter, shea butter, coconut oil, and castor oil, and combine in a heat-safe container. Carefully warm to between 160 and 170 degrees Fahrenheit.

3. If using glycerin and fragrance or essential oil, measure these now and set them aside for Step 7.

4. Measure the correct amounts of both lyes (potassium hydroxide and sodium hydroxide) into an appropriate container, and measure the correct amount of water into a separate container. Carefully add the lye to the water, stirring gently and thoroughly. Stir until solution is clear.

5. When lye water is between 150 and 180 degrees Fahrenheit, slowly pour lye water into oils/butters.

6. Use a stick blender to mix until the lye water and the oils are completely combined. Your mixture may be thick (mashed potato-like) almost instantly, or it may take up to a minute for the mixture to pull together and become homogeneous.

7. Stir in glycerin and fragrance (if using). Continue stirring by hand until these additives are well-incorporated and the mixture does not separate. Be careful not to stir too quickly or vigorously, as the glycerin may cause the batter to slosh or slide around in the container initially.

8. Continue stirring until soap reaches a thinned-out, Vaseline-type stage. Temperature, fragrance, and essential oil can each have varying

effects on the consistency of the soap at this stage. If your soap does not become thinned-out and shiny, allow it to rest for a few minutes and then stir again. If it stays thick, proceed with the next step.

9. Depending on the thickness of your mixture, either pour or scoop the soap into a mold or heat-safe containers. Be sure to verify that the temperature tolerances of the containers or mold are appropriate for high-heat mixtures. (Containers labeled PP are one safe option.) Gently tap containers on a firm surface to help reduce air pockets.

10. If pouring into individual containers/tubs, allow the soap to cool completely before covering. Placing lids on the containers too early may create excessive moisture or high temperatures.

Recipe 8 LOG

Date:

Notes:

Recipe 9

A variation on the typical ingredients, with lard forming the foundation for this concoction.

Oils/Fat	%	Ounces	Grams
Stearic acid	35%	11.2	318
Lard	35%	11.2	318
Cocoa Butter	10%	3.2	91
Shea Butter	10%	3.2	91
Coconut Oil	5%	1.6	45
Castor Oil	5%	1.6	45
Lyes			
Potassium hydroxide (KOH)	60%	4	113
Sodium Hydroxide (NaOH)	40%	1.7	48
Other			
Distilled water		12.15	344
Glycerin (optional)		3.2	90
Fragrance (optional)		1-1.4	28-40

Gather all necessary equipment, tools, containers, and ingredients before beginning, and prepare your work area. Read through the entire recipe and instructions prior to starting the soapmaking process.

1. Suit up! When making soap, always wear goggles, gloves, closed-toe shoes, and long sleeves.

2. Measure the correct amount of stearic acid, lard, cocoa butter, shea

butter, coconut oil, and castor oil. Combine the oils/fats and carefully warm to between 160 and 170 degrees Fahrenheit.

3. If using glycerin and fragrance or essential oil, measure these now and set them aside for Step 7.

4. Measure the correct amounts of lyes and water into appropriate containers. Carefully add the lye to the water, stirring gently and thoroughly, until solution is clear.

5. When lye water is between 150 and 180 degrees Fahrenheit, slowly pour lye water into oils/butters.

6. Using a stick blender, mix until the lye water and the oils are completely combined. Your mixture may take a minute or two to fully combine and become homogeneous, or it may be thick almost instantly.

7. Stir in glycerin and fragrance (if using). Continue stirring by hand until these additives are well-incorporated and the mixture does not separate. Be careful not to stir too quickly or vigorously, as the glycerin may cause the batter to slosh or slide around in the container initially.

8. Continue stirring until soap reaches a smooth, thinner consistency. This is typically anywhere from 2-10 minutes. Temperature, fragrance, and essential oil can each have varying effects on the consistency of the soap at this stage. If your soap does not become thinned-out and shiny,

allow it to rest for a few minutes and then stir again. If it stays thick, proceed with the next step.

9. Depending on the thickness of your mixture, either pour or scoop the soap into a mold or heat-safe containers. Be sure to verify that the temperature tolerances of the containers or mold are appropriate for high-heat mixtures. (Containers labeled PP are one safe option.) Gently tap containers on a firm surface to help reduce air pockets.

10. If pouring into individual containers/tubs, allow the soap to cool completely before covering. Placing lids on the containers too early may create excessive moisture or high temperatures.

Recipe 9 LOG

Date:

Notes:

Recipe 10			
A recipe featuring lard, but letting the stearic acid shine.			
Oils/Fat	**%**	**Ounces**	**Grams**
Stearic acid	50%	16	454
Lard	25%	8	227
Cocoa Butter	15%	4.8	136
Shea Butter	5%	1.6	45
Coconut Oil	5%	1.6	45
Lyes			
Potassium hydroxide (KOH)	60%	4	113
Sodium Hydroxide (NaOH)	40%	1.7	48
Other			
Distilled water		12.15	344
Glycerin (optional)		3.2	90
Fragrance (optional)		1-1.4	28-40

Before beginning, prepare your soaping area and gather all necessary equipment, tools, containers, and ingredients. Read through the entire recipe and instructions prior to starting the soapmaking process.

1. Suit up! When making soap, always wear goggles, gloves, closed-toe shoes, and long sleeves.

2. Measure the correct amount of all oils and fats (stearic acid, lard, cocoa butter, shea butter, and coconut oil). Combine the oils/fats and carefully warm to between 160 and 170 degrees Fahrenheit.

3. If using glycerin and fragrance or essential oil, measure these now and set them aside for Step 7.

4. Measure out the correct amounts of potassium hydroxide (KOH) and sodium hydroxide (NaOH) into an appropriate container; measure out the correct amount of water into a separate container. Carefully add the lye to the water, stirring gently and thoroughly until the solution is clear.

5. When lye water is between 150 and 180 degrees Fahrenheit, slowly pour lye water into oils/butters.

6. Use a stick blender (and stirring, if necessary) to mix until the lye water and the oils are completely combined. Your mixture may become thick quickly, or it may take up to a minute or more for the mixture to pull together and become homogeneous.

7. Stir in glycerin and fragrance (if using). Continue stirring by hand until these additives are well-incorporated and the mixture does not separate. (If you stir too quickly or vigorously, the glycerin may cause the batter to slosh or slide around in the container initially.)

8. Continue stirring until soap becomes thinner and smoother. This is typically anywhere from 2-10 minutes. Temperature, fragrance, and essential oil can each have varying effects on the consistency of the soap at this stage. If your soap does not become thinned-out and shiny,

allow it to rest for a few minutes and then stir again. If it stays thick, proceed with the next step.

9. Before filling containers or molds, be sure to verify that the temperature tolerances of the units are appropriate for high-heat mixtures. (Containers labeled PP are one safe option.) Depending on the thickness of your mixture, either pour or scoop the soap into your containers. Gently tap containers on a firm surface to help reduce air pockets.

10. If pouring into individual containers/tubs, allow the soap to cool completely before covering. Placing lids on the containers too early may create excessive moisture or high temperatures.

Recipe 10 LOG

Date:

Notes:

CHAPTER 10

ARRIVAL:
Beyond the Land of Lather

Congratulations on arriving at your destination, the Land of Lather! You've got a high quality shaving soap now, and it's almost time to put it to work as your ticket into the wider World of Wet Shaving. But before you go any farther, it's vitally important to take time and test your creation. Hopefully you've tried the soap yourself and love it. Share it with a group of experienced wet shavers and ask for their candid feedback. Noting details such as the hardness/softness of their water, whether they bowl lather or face lather, how many passes they make, their personal level of skin sensitivity, etc. will assist you in deciding if you should press on with this formula or take a few steps back to adjust the sails.

As I mentioned earlier, wet shaving communities really have a culture of their own. Respect their society by getting to know the natives (and their ways) before trying to sell your wares to them. You can develop meaningful communication and connections with wet shavers through social media, online groups, and forums, as well as live events. (For a list of groups and forums to get you started, see the Appendix.) Also, don't be afraid to reach out within your current sphere of influence (friends, family, and customers) and ask for a show of hands of those who enjoy wet shaving. You might be surprised at the results. The more you know about the traditional shaving and those who embrace it, the better you'll be able to relate to and meet the needs of those who want what you've got. Instead of being just a visitor in Wet Shaving World, you might even decide to stake a claim and settle in. Happy Sailing!

CHAPTER 11
NAVIGATING HEAVY SEAS:
Troubleshooting

My hope is that the information in this book has assisted you in making a shaving soap that you're proud to sell. While I've tried to anticipate hang-ups and obstacles you might encounter, there's a good chance you might have hit a snag or two along the way. If you experience some heavy seas, use the following charts to calm the water.

Problems During Production		
Problem	**Cause**	**Solution**
Instant trace after adding lye water	High stearic content	This is typical and not of concern. Continue to blend or stir, and soap will loosen up and thin somewhat.
Too thick to mix	High stearic content	If using a stick blender, try stirring by hand. Additionally, check temperature. If the mixture is 150 degrees Fahrenheit or below, try adding a small amount of heat to warm the batter.

Problems During Production		
Problem	**Cause**	**Solution**
Mixture seems watery	Low stearic content	Allow the mixture to sit for a few minutes to see if it will thicken. You can also try stirring or stick blending to see if there is any change.
	Ingredient measured incorrectly	Start over.
Mixture rises or creates a volcano when lye water is added to the oils	Temperature of oils or lye water is too high	Stir, stir, stir! Many times the mixture can be stirred down and contained. If the soap creeps out of the container onto your working surface, you can continue working with what is left in the mixing vessel, if you will not be adding any more ingredients. If you will be using additives, it is best to start over so that your proportions are accurate.

Problems With the Finished Product		
Problem	Cause	Solution
Lather doesn't last	Not enough stearic content	Reformulate, increasing the stearic/palmitic content either by using a higher percentage of stearic acid as an ingredient or adding/increasing butters that are high in stearic and palmitic acid.
Lather is too thin	Too much water was used when creating a lather	Start lathering again with a dryer brush.
	Not enough stearic content	Reformulate as described above in "Lather doesn't last" section.
Lather doesn't provide good cushion	Weak/thin lather	Rework the lather with a drier brush.
	Too much stearic content	Increase (or add) fats and/or butters to your recipe.

Problems with the Finished Product		
Problem	**Cause**	**Solution**
Leaves skin feeling dried out	Not enough moisturizing or humectant properties in recipe	Add up to 10% glycerin to the recipe. Increase the amount of oleic acid in the formulation by a small amount.
Soap leaves a warming or burning sensation on skin	Lye heavy	Throw out the soap and start again.
	FO heavy	Throw out the soap and start again.
	Ingredient irritation	Reformulate your recipe.
Difficult to lather	This could be a variety of factors, from the formulation to the lathering technique.	Have someone else try to lather the soap. If they are having difficulty creating a good lather, examine your recipe to see if it is formulated with the desirable characteristics.

Problems With the Finished Product		
Problem	**Cause**	**Solution**
Soap looks "mottled" or has white spots.	Most likely these are stearic spots, due to soaping at cooler temperature. Can also be lye spots.	Test the spots to see if they zap. If not, there is no need for concern. Eliminate the spots on the next batch by soaping at a slightly higher temperature.

APPENDIX

Stake Your Claim in the Land of Lather

Making shaving soap is one thing; convincing people to purchase it is another. Your first step, of course, is to create a killer soap. If you've read this book thoroughly and followed the principles given, that shouldn't be a problem.

Your next steps toward selling, then, should be focused on knowing both your product and the wet shaving community in a way that enables you to interact and connect with potential customers in an authentic, educated manner. The articles included in this Appendix will assist and equip you to achieve that goal.

How to Lather a Shaving Brush

Knowing how to lather a shaving brush isn't rocket science, but it does take a bit of practice to get it right. The following steps will get you started on the right path.

1. Soak the bristles of the shaving brush in warm or hot water. (A synthetic brush does not require this step.)

2. If you have a medium-hard or hard soap, add a layer of hot water to the top of the soap and allow it to soak for about 1-3 minutes. If you have a soft (easily pressable) soap, you will probably want to skip this step.

3. Squeeze or shake out excess water from the shaving brush, so that you're left with a slightly damp brush. If you have a synthetic brush, run it quickly under hot water to dampen it, and squeeze out any excess water.

4. Pour water off the top of the soap.

5. Take the damp brush and load soap by swirling shaving brush in a circular motion over the surface of the soap for approximately 30-45 seconds.

6. Wet your face lightly.

7. Take the loaded brush to your face (if face lathering) or to a palm-sized bowl (if bowl lathering) and swirl in a circular motion, allowing the lather to build.

8. Add drops of water as needed (a little at a time) to the tips of the brush and continue to swirl to build lather, until you have a thick, rich, creamy lather that resembles shaving cream/whipped topping. Final lather that is shave-ready should have a wet sheen to it, without being watery or containing lots of micro bubble.

Shaving Forums/Groups

Get involved! The best way to know what wet shavers want is to hang out with them on a regular basis. An additional benefit is that they'll get to know you better and when they're ready to search out a new shaving soap to try, they'll know where to turn.

Badger & Blade (B&B): Badgerandblade.com

The Shave Nook (TSN): Shavenook.com

The Shave Den (TSD): Theshaveden.com/forums

Reddit: Reddit.com/r/wicked_edge/and Reddit.com/r/Wetshaving/

Facebook Groups:

Razor & Brush

Shave the Man

The BiG Shave

The Wet Shaving Society

Wet Shaver Review.

Acronyms of Wet Shaving

The lingo in the wet shaving world can be a challenge initially and even more so when they throw in all the fabulous acronyms. Keep this list handy and you won't be intimidated when you read about someone's advice to use SC and go ATG to get a CCS during their SOTD.

Most Important / Most Often Used:

BBS – Baby Butt Smooth

SOTD – Shave of the Day

General Acronymns:

AS – After Shave

ASB – Aftershave Balm

ATG – Against the Grain

CCS – Close Comfortable Shave

CWR – Cold Water Rinse

CWS – Cold Water Shave

EdC – Eau de Cologne

EdP – Eau de Parfum

EdT – Eau de Toilette

FTB – Feel The Burn

FWIW – For What It's Worth

HTT – How Towel Treatment

LE – Limited Edition

PSO – Pre-Shave Oil

SAS – Socially Acceptable Shave (can include light stubble)

SC – Shaving Cream (or Soap Commander)

SS – Shaving Soap

SWMBO – She Who Must Be Obeyed

WTG – With the Grain

WWR – Warm Water Rinse

XTG – Across the Grain

YMMV – Your Mileage May Vary

The "Acquisition Disorders":

BAD – Brush Acquisition Disorder

RAD – Razor Acquisition Disorder

RBAD – Razor Blade Acquisition Disorder

SAD – Soap Acquisition Disorder

SBAD – Shaving Brush Acquisition Disorder

SSAD – Shaving Soap Acquisition Disorder

Types of Razors:

CC – Closed Comb

DE – Double Edge

DOC – Double Open Comb

OC – Open Comb

SE – Single Edge

SR – Straight Razor

TTO – Twist to Open

Shaving Soaps/Companies:

AoS – Art of Shaving

B&M – Barrister & Mann

CB – Catie's Bubbles

CRSW – Cold River Soap Works

GG – Ginger's Garden

MBS – Mama Bear Soaps

MdC – Martin de Candre

MLS – Mickey Lee Soapworks

MWF – Mitchell's Wool Fat (also called The Fat)

PAA – Phoenix Artisan Accoutrements

RR – RazoRock

SC – Soap Commander

T&H – Truefitt & Hill

TOBS – Taylor of Old Bond Street

Benefits of Traditional Wet Shaving

Wet shaving is a booming industry, and with good reason. More and more men (and women) are discovering that the novelty of wet shaving is accompanied by a good number of benefits. Ask a seasoned wet shaver and he or she is likely to come up with a few more to add to this list.

1. A closer shave. Electric razors can't cut nearly as close as a razor blade! Likewise, cartridges and disposable razors can't hold a candle to the shave you can achieve with a traditional razor.

2. A more comfortable shave. When done well, a traditional shave provides an easy and enjoyable experience, free of tugs, nicks, and burns. Good technique + stellar shave soap = fabulous feel.

3. It's cheaper. The initial investment in wet shaving "gear" (razors, blades, brushes, and soaps) may seem like a big chunk of change at the outset, but most of these are one-time purchases (except for the blades and soaps). You really only need one decent-quality razor and one good-quality brush to get the job done; no fancy gear is required. (Need more convincing about the cost? Check out the current prices on the disposable cartridge replacement blades.)

4. It slows you down. At first glance this may not seem like a desirable characteristic, but once you make the habit of setting aside time for a relaxing, enjoyable shave you'll begin to miss it on those mornings when you have to rush out the door.

5. Environmentalism. Disposable razors, cartridges, and shaving cans all end up in landfills. With traditional wet shaving the only hardware you're disposing of on a regular basis is razor blades (which can actually be recycled in some areas). And for the ultra-environmentalist there are straight razors. Almost zero waste!

6. Less irritation. Most men who suffer from sensitive or easily-irritated skin find that this style of shaving provides a more comfortable experience, both during and after the shave.

7. The thrill. There's not a better way to live life "on the edge" while shaving than by gliding a finely-honed straight razor across your neck.

8. The tradition. Not too many generations ago words like "disposable" and "cartridges" were never used in conjunction with shaving. Authentic, traditional wet shaving is associated with a classic, simpler time in life and many men desire to continue that legacy for their own selves and their sons.

9. Community. Not everyone on the block is a wet shaver, but the number is steadily growing. Though it may seem quirky to outsiders, wet shaving creates an almost instant connection among men who share the hobby. The bond supersedes most cultural, religious, economic, and, yes, political differences.

10. Fun. Yes, most wet shavers will tell you that they have fun shaving. And that they look forward to shaving. That they actually plan out their shaves and, sometimes, take pictures of their set-ups. (Don't believe me? Google "shave of the day" and see what comes up.)

Benefits of Handcrafted Shaving Soap

Handcrafted shaving soap isn't a necessity to wet shaving, but it sure does kick it up a notch. Being able to engage your customers in the benefits of purchasing something handmade by you (as opposed to a commodity that comes from the factory) can move them from leery to loyal in no time.

1. Impact. Buying handmade means you're directly supporting an artisan, and making an impact on his/her family, rather than a large scale corporation. It's an investment into the maker, both personally and professionally.

2. Ingredients. All it takes is a quick glance at the label of an artisan shaving soap to see the richness of what's inside. Most handcrafted shaving soaps contain considerably more nourishing and skin-friendly ingredients than their chemicals-in-a-can cousins.

3. Interaction. Have a question about how the soap is made? Want to know the best way to store the product between uses? Curious about why a certain ingredient is included? Just ask the artisan. Most handcrafters relish the opportunity to answer questions, create connections, share tips, and educate customers on their product and its benefits.

4. Interesting Aromas. Commercial shaving companies are selective in their scent offerings, but handmade shaving soap doesn't suffer from the same olfactory limits. The variety of fragrances available for a maker to use in creating shaving products is practically infinite. Boring and repetitive are not in most artisans' vocabulary.

5. Inspiration. Scents can take us places, from far-away, exotic destinations to summer nights on the front porch, from holidays spent at grandma's house to a whiff of a loved-one's special perfume. Not every jar of shaving soap will evoke a special memory, but don't be surprised when you find yourself lost in a shave.

6. Indulgence. Every once in a while it's nice to get something "just because", but many times those indulgences leave a larger-than-expected hole in our wallet. Not so with handcrafted shaving soaps. Most artisans take care to price their products at levels that are fair to both them and their customers, making their soaps an affordable, everyday luxury.

Additional Men's Grooming Products

As your customers become hooked on your shaving soap, they'll be asking you for more products in their favorite scent. Consider adding a few of these handcrafted items to your offerings:

Aftershave Balm

Aftershave Milk

Aftershave Splash

Bath Soap

Beard Balm

Beard Oil

Beard Soap

Body Lotion

Body Spray

Body Wash

Deodorant

Lip Balm

Pomade

Pre-Shave Oil

Shampoo & Conditioner

Shampoo Bar

Prevent Ingrown Hairs & Razor Bumps

The following article is a blog post I wrote to address a problem that plagues many men. I'm including it here so that you'll be better equipped to understand and address the needs of your shaving customers.

Many men experience ingrown hairs or razor bumps while shaving. Medically known as *pseudofolliculitis barbae*, this condition occurs when a hair grows out of the skin, curls around, and grows back in (razor bump) or the hair grows back after shaving but doesn't exit the follicle, getting trapped underneath the skin (ingrown hair). Either way...OUCH! In both situations, hairs that are lodged in the skin can cause inflammation and appear as tender, itchy, red, raised bumps (many times being mistaken for acne). And men with coarse or curly hair are more prone to dealing with the challenges of these wayward hairs.

That's the frustrating news. But the good news is that traditional wet shaving offers some easy steps you can take to prevent or reduce the incidences of ingrown hairs and razor bumps. And the doubly good news is that I'm into alliteration, so you just have to remember a few *S's* to get you on the right track.

Quick Note: The following recommendations apply specifically to shaving with Single Edge or Double Edge razors and may not be as applicable for Straight Razor users, especially the information pertaining to stretching the skin. As with most recommendations, your mileage may vary, depending on your specific skin and hair type.

How to Prevent or Reduce Ingrown Hairs and Razor Bumps:

1. SCRUB (lightly). Many men find that using a gently exfoliating scrub or cleanser helps to remove the dead layer of skin that can clog the hair follicles. Doing this seems to encourage hair growth in the right direction, while moisturizing the hair that is about to be shaved.

2. SOAK & SOFTEN. Wetting the beard with warm water for 2-5 minutes before shaving allows the hair to be more pliant and easier to cut than dry hair. If you shower first, this is an easy step that you're already doing. If you don't shower before shaving, try applying a warm, wet towel or washcloth to hydrate your skin and whiskers.

3. SOAP (or cream). Choose a good quality shaving soap or cream that will provide plenty of cushion and glide, to make the razor pass more smoothly and also create a more comfortable situation for inflamed skin. Allowing the shaving soap to sit on the skin for a little bit before shaving may also help to soften and moisturize the hair, further reducing friction and irritation.

4. SHAVE SIMPLY. This isn't the place to get all fancy and try some new tricks. Simply go WITH the grain (WTG) of your hair growth and try to take fewer strokes. Additionally, allow the skin to remain in a neutral, relaxed position (no stretching...we'll explain why later on in this post). WTG, few strokes, and relaxed skin will reduce the chance of cutting the hair below the surface of the skin, which can lead to a greater risk of ingrown hairs.

5. SPOIL YOUR SKIN. Immediately after shaving, be sure to rinse thoroughly, preferably with cold water. Following up with a good quality aftershave or moisturizer will help keep your skin healthy between shaves and better prepped for your next shaving session.

Two bonus *S's* regarding your blade:

- **SHARP.** Shave with a sharp blade. A dull blade doesn't cut as easily, meaning you'll be more tempted to go back over that area to try to get closer. It can also result in uneven tearing of the hair. Remember also to rinse the blade after each pass which helps remove skin and hair that gets caught in the blade. This creates a better set-up for smoother, less irritating shaving. Additionally, know when to throw the blade away, usually after 3-5 uses (depending on the blade).

- **SINGLE.** Stay away from multi-blade razors that can lift and cut hair below the natural, relaxed skin line.

And finally, why NOT to stretch the skin while shaving: Pulling or stretching the skin causes the hair to raise up (protrude) above the natural level of the skin. When the skin is released, hair can then "pop back" to below skin level. The skin then covers the hair, essentially trapping it underneath and not allowing it to grow easily out of the follicle. End result? Ingrown hairs.

RESOURCES

SOAPMAKING BOOKS

Start with one of these books to learn the basics of soapmaking:

Pure Soapmaking: How to Create Nourishing, Natural Skin Care Soaps by Anne-Marie Faiola

Smart Soapmaking by Anne L. Watson

Soap Crafting: Step-by-Step Techniques for Making 31 Unique Cold-Process Soaps, by Anne-Marie Faiola and Lara Ferroni

The Everything Soapmaking Book, 2nd Edition, by Alicia Grosso.

The Soapmaker's Companion by Susan Miller Cavitch

FATTY ACID PROFILE CHARTS

Go Native:
gonative.co.nz/Resources/Table+of+fatty+acid+content+of+oils+for+soapmaking.html

Nature's Garden:
Naturesgardencandles.com/mas_assets/theme/ngc/pdf/soapoils.pdf

The Soap Dish: Thesoapdish.com/oil-properties-chart.htm

ONLINE LYE CALCULATORS

Bramble Berry: brambleberry.com/Pages/Lye-Calculator.aspx
NOTE: To generate the KOH amount, select "Liquid" for the type of soap. To obtain the NaOH amount, select "Solid" soap.

Majestic Mountain Sage (calculates dual lyes):
Thesage.com/calcs/LyeCalc.html

NOTE: When using this lye calculator, you do not input superfat or use percentages for oils/fats. Instead, input the specific quantities (ounces, pounds, or grams) of your oils/fats, and the program will generate the percentages of these ingredients, along with the quantities of each lye needed for various levels of superfat.

SoapCalc: Soapcalc.net/calc/soapcalcwp.asp

SUPPLIERS

Containers for shaving soap

Bramble Berry: Brambleberry.com

Container & Packaging Supply: Containerandpackaging.com

Freund Container & Supply: Freundcontainer.com

McKernan Packaging Clearing House: Mckernan.com

Nature's Garden: Naturesgardencandles.com

Parkway Plastics, Inc.: Parkwayjars.com

SKS Bottle & Packaging, Inc.: Sks-bottle.com

The Cary Company: Thecarycompany.com

Wholesale Supplies Plus: Wholesalesuppliesplus.com

Lye

Duda Diesel: Dudadiesel.com

Essential Depot: Essentialdepot.com

Oils/Butters

Bramble Berry: Brambleberry.com

Elements Bath & Body: Elementsbathandbody.com

Essential Wholesale & Labs: Essentialwholesale.com

Jedwards International, Inc.: Bulknaturaloils.com

Nature's Garden: Naturesgardencandles.com

Rustic Escentuals: Rusticescentuals.com

Soapers Choice (Columbus Foods): Soaperschoice.com

Wholesale Supplies Plus: Wholesalesuppliesplus.com

Fragrances & Essential Oils
There are many reputable sources of fragrance and essential oils. The ones listed here are just a sampling:

Bramble Berry: Brambleberry.com

Elements Bath & Body: Elementsbathandbody.com

Essential Wholesale & Labs: Essentialwholesale.com

Lebermuth Co.: Lebermuth.com/

Liberty Natural Products: Libertynatural.com

MAD Oils: Madoils.com

Nature's Garden: Naturesgardencandles.com

New Directions Aromatics: Newdirectionsaromatics.com

Rustic Escentuals: Rusticescentuals.com

Wholesale Supplies Plus: Wholesalesuppliesplus.com

<u>Shaving Hardware</u>

Italian Barber: Italianbarber.com

Maggard Razors: Maggardrazors.com

Phoenix Artisan Accoutrements: Phoenixartisanaccoutrements.com

Q Brothers: Qbrothers.com

Razor Emporium: Razoremporium.com

The Old Town Shaving Company: Oldtownshaving.com

West Coast Shaving: Westcoastshaving.com

ONLINE HELPS FOR MAKING SHAVING SOAPS

Shaver Soaper: Shaversoaper.com

Two helpful Kevin Devine videos include:
Experiments with Shaving Soap (testing KOH & NaOH ratios and percentage of Stearic Acid): Youtube.com/watch?v=L5UxMNatAyY

Making and cutting a hot process shaving soap:
Youtube.com/watch?v=prS8rx2x5dg

ABOUT THE AUTHOR

Carrie Seibert is a Certified Soapmaker and member of the Handcrafted Soap & Cosmetics Guild. She is also an active Board member of the Alabama Soap & Candle Association. In 2014, she and her husband, Darren, founded Soap Commander—a handcrafted men's grooming company that empowers men through the traditional art of wet shaving.

Carrie, Darren, and their 7 children savor a lifestyle of learning in northern Alabama. When she's not homeschooling or making soap, Carrie enjoys connecting with her children and strengthening her marriage. Her best days begin with a morning run, end with a great book, and contain lots of hummus in-between.

ACKNOWLEDGMENTS

A very special thanks to:

My husband Darren, who spent precious time helping me craft and shape my thoughts. I'm so glad you don't panic when we go for long car rides armed with steno pads, highlighters, and folders stuffed full of random notes and half-finished ideas.

My sons, who will make fabulous husbands one day. You guys have nearly perfected the elusive skill of reading a woman's non-verbal clues and responding appropriately.

My daughters, who infallibly make my heart smile with their exceptional hugs and radiant joy. Thank you for allowing sporadic snippets of "girl time" to sustain and strengthen us over these past few months. I love to watch each of you shine!

Kayla Fioravanti, my faithful and fearless editor and friend. Your patience, prayers, and sincere support during a most difficult season in the life of our family enabled me to peacefully pursue the completion of this project amidst some swirling seas. What a joy to know that we both have the same Anchor.

Donna Maria Coles Johnson, founder and leader of the Indie Business Network. Your relentless enthusiasm, encouragement, and empowerment of entrepreneurs in the handcrafted industry is making a difference in thousands of lives, including mine, every single day. Thank you for gently handing me the tools I need to create a life I love.

The soapmaking community as a whole—including the Handcrafted Soap & Cosmetics Guild—for journeying together in the pursuit of knowledge and art. Specifically, friends such as Irena Marchu (Ginger's Garden) and Chris Cullen (Catie's Bubbles) played critical roles in helping me build a solid foundation in cold process soapmaking and later steering me in the right direction as I entered the arena of shaving soaps. You two have set the bar high.

Last (but really first), my Lord and Savior, Jesus Christ. Any good in me is from Him and Him alone.

Made in the USA
Las Vegas, NV
24 February 2021